House Fire

A Collection of Poems by B. J. Buhrow

1990 Minnesota Voices Project Winner

NEW RIVERS PRESS 1992

Library of Congress Catalog Card Number 91-61254
ISBN 0-89823-129-9

Edited by Vivian Vie Balfour
Editorial Assistance by Paul J. Hintz
Cover collage by Dave Dentinger
Book Design by Gaylord Schanilec
Typesetting by Peregrine Publications

Some of the poems in *House Fire* originally appeared, in somewhat different versions, in the following publications: *Abraxas, Blue Unicorn, The Cape Rock, Feminist Voices, The Madison Review, The Minnesota Review, Mississippi Valley Review of Creative Writing, Passages North, Wisconsin Academy Review,* and *The Wisconsin Review*. Our thanks to the editors of these publications for allowing us to reprint the works here.

The publication of *House Fire: A Collection of Poems* has been made possible by grants from the Jerome Foundation and the Metropolitan Regional Arts Council (from an appropriation by the Minnesota Legislature). Additional support has been provided by the Arts Development Fund of the United Arts Council, the First Bank System Foundation, Liberty State Bank, the Star Tribune/Cowles Media Company, the Tennant Company Foundation, and the National Endowment for the Arts (with funds appropriated by the Congress of the United States). New Rivers Press also wishes to acknowledge the Minnesota Non-Profits Assistance Fund for its invaluable support.

New Rivers Press books are distributed by

The Talman Company
150 Fifth Avenue
New York, NY 10011

Bookslinger
2402 University Avenue West
Saint Paul, MN 55114

House Fire: A Collection of Poems has been manufactured in the United States of America for New Rivers Press, 420 N. 5th Street/Suite 910, Minneapolis, MN 55401 in a first edition of 1,200 copies.

For my daughter, Roxanne, with all my love, and for David, with all my love and a little spit.

CONTENTS

One

Two

Three

One

House Fire

Parents talked
in nudges and rushes, water
hung in the air
like yellow crepe paper,

everything was late and loose,
kids, dogs, the falling
walls of a house,
the bitter

chocolate smell of burning
made me starve
for something, I pulled
at my mother's skirts.

She was surrounding
another woman with her arms.
The bright cloth
crawled out of my hands.

The Shining Money of Love

We wear small white handkerchiefs
on our bent heads, the wings of angels
to bear our baby sins up to heaven.
The bright stained glass lights tug us
into the pew. We are good, good girls,
only twigs in the tree, but still
fine wood. God's son was a carpenter,
so He can tell. When the choir files in,
He looks into our hearts, lifts
the lids of the small hinged boxes
and, seeing the shining money
of love inside, begins to sing.

Murderer

In the back yard up north
blanket over a clothesline
my cousin's tent
the night has fewer lights
in it than I am used to
it smells of the nearby river
we are telling stories for the dark

I come up with the legendary babysitter
on the phone, the maniac
on the upstairs extension bouncing
a baby's head like a ball
then my cousin, hunched
solemnly over the flashlight fire
says now this is real, it happened
here, and tells me how

Buck Bannerman saw the house
at first it looked like any
thrifty hunter's, then closer
there were girls hung
from hooks, headless, their bodies
gutted like deer
chairs upholstered with skin
fingers packed in a pickle jar

you know Buck, she says
that big fat sheriff?
he had the dry heaves for weeks
lost fifty pounds, then she sees
how white my face is, and tries
to bully me out of being sick
he's not here stupid
they locked him up in Waupun,
but the thick air
is bearing down, monsters

are being born who shuffle
through the subdued streets
of this small town, the look
in my cousin's eyes as I run
into the house, tell
Grandma what she's done.

Carny

As we watch him work under
the glow on the wooden
platform, he is beautifully
bored, his greasy denim vest
skims the bared muscles
of his chest like fancy
chains he could break
with one dangerous thought,

and we nuzzle each other
forward through the hot
sticky night, giggling
like a drink of cold
clear water while he looks
us over with a blue flick
of his cigarette into the dirt
and takes our tickets
in his hard hands, then

we are up in the air knowing
he hears us and the louder
we are the longer he'll keep us
in these big mechanical
unyielding arms, so we shriek
until we can't breathe,
until our screams are perfect.

The Abortion

On that sudden trip to New York
we stayed with my mom's friend
Lynn and her kids. Their house
was near the Hudson and Mom left
for the city while we played
on its banks, and time slipped past me.
All at once I missed her
so deeply that I couldn't ask
these strangers where she was.
At dusk when she came back

and sat with Lynn on the porch
drinking, I fought
with the other kids over some
broken rule and her voice
was clear and sharp
in the warm air like ice rattling
against what would never melt
as she called out to me,
don't complain. I walked off

stiff with my loss
of the game in such tricky
light, the same light
that was making my mother
look so young, turning
the gin in her glass pink
as a blush or a drop
of blood in the river
growing thinner, washing away.

Monarch Butterflies

During the usual dinner table argument,
fidgeting on the edge
of adolescence, I look out
at the huge maple in the back yard, it is
covered with monarch butterflies, dozens
and dozens like unimaginable leaves,

and their flutter is suddenly everywhere,
even in my vegetable soup: the brown broth
with sluggish detestable carrots
grows quick patterns
and beautifies my spoon,

while my mother's face softens
into a sweet excited flush
with dark eyelashes, she whispers
"wonderful," and there is no more
loud hard talk during supper,
nothing to dislodge those fragile wings.

Rain: Sunday School for the Deaf and Blind

It is Palm
Sunday. The boy smells rain
outside the schoolroom.
He begins to dream

of a sunny day, no rain
beside a deep lake.
Like a dream
a fish moves

through the dark, silent lake
towards a sharp hook.
The fish moves.
The boy feels the tug

on the sharp hook
of a huge death.
The boy feels the tug
on his hand, rousing him

with the story of a huge death,
the weight like endless rain
on his hand, rousing him
to Jesus, Jesus

the weight of rain
and love. Sunday: someone drums
a lesson about Jesus
into his palm.

"Mental Patient Mauled by Polar Bear in Vilas Park Zoo"

Father stood in the doorway
staring at me benignly
in his white shirt and big body

his shirt as white as snow
the kind you can eat safely
the kind that keeps angels

the kind that could fall
on the moon, the kind like fur
and his body was as big as a bear

the comic kind, the kind
you feel sorry for
as it waves its paws

far behind the railings
framed by bare rock
after the storm

of marshmallows begins
and I taste iron in my mouth
and my feet grow wings.

Cemetery

When we were smaller, silk ladies
would show up at my Grandma's door
and say, Lucille, your wild grandkids
were out on those graves again,
playing. And Grandma would say
jump on my grave all day long when I'm dead
kids and tell them I told you to.
My second cousin Bucky took after her,
was the town bad boy and I followed him
through all the weeds of childhood
into the cemetery until I was thirteen
and we stood in the shade
of the Crawford headstone, pirating
married names from the dead.
His kiss tipped the summer on its side,
a prank bordering on crime
and in the dark loose dirt of walking home
when cars black with mourners edged
up the gravel road, I burrowed and hid
from Grandma's death, Bucky's wildness
and my own surviving
like granite sunk into the untended
green grass of their eyes.

Piñata

The fat pink paper-mache burro
is strung up in the branches.
Its secrets are all sweet
inside it. Blindfolded,
a small boy swings a stick,
and of course misses, and all
morning the children keep
missing, even the birthday girl
for whom the burro, if it
was docile, would surely
give birth. Finally, the daddy
has to take a knife
to its belly. The candy
rains straight down, then
dresses are torn, knees
bruised, and no one can
kiss away the injustice
of the strongest getting
the most. Sunset endows
the exhausted body of the burro
with the blushes of someone
hanged for the wrong crime.

Red Kimono

He was never away that long
or traveled that far
but one night my father
did bring home a red kimono
for my mother, and she put it on
and danced and bowed
and shooed my sister and me to bed.

We saw the kimono one more time.
At a New Year's party,
when my mother tucked
her black hair under a blacker wig
and painted her face
as white as crepe paper.
Late that night, my sister and I walked
on our small, soundless feet
to the head of the stairs

and there in the thread
of light over the bar
my father stood,
and in the debris of the party,
my mother sat, and the sleeve
of the kimono was ripped apart
at the shoulder so
we could see the skin
between the edges of the red gown.

Downtown

We are out late without
our parents knowing.
Jailbait. We jangle
our bracelets, catch
the marquee light once
on a charm that's shaped
like a ship. Pretend
it's a big diamond. Then
a sailor with eyes like two
blue bowls, something
sharp swimming inside them,
breaks away from his buddies,
makes a barricade with his hands
and the movie house, makes a woman
open up on his arm muscle.
We blush and he jumps
back laughing and the street
is a frenzy of white uniforms.

There Was a War Going On

they hung on to high school, warm
brief summers drumming
on any surface with two fingers

prettier than girls
bending, outlined, sudden
in their baggy clothes

blissful over something small,
a sharp car, a game of pool
they made geography

seem cruel
but they had to be taught everything
those boys

sweet, and slight, and young
they melted like candy on the tongue

The Lesson

I go out to the bars
with this girl named Colleen.
We don't have money,
so we hitchhike. A car

stops. We get in.
One of the men in the front seat
turns. His eyes drill into us.
He pulls out a gun

and says get undressed.
The driver starts to drive
faster. All the lights
from the closed stores press

up against the car windows
and blur. Colleen digs
her fingers into my leg,
begins to talk like she knows

these men, kids with them.
The gun is a good joke.
All three laugh. The gun
is lowered, the driving calms

down, the car stops. They let us
out. Be more careful
next time, girls, one calls
back. On the street,

Colleen turns toward
me, points at the tears
on my face, says you almost
got us killed. Then slaps me, hard.

Pretty

When Charlene, my homely friend,
was in an old car that stopped dead
on railroad tracks, she was able
to jump, roll down the embankment
and live on, with a long
facial scar and a limp.

I wonder if I would have taken
that leap like her, down
a slick, disfiguring slope,
stones scraping off makeup
and then skin. Or would
I have waited, stalled
in my prettiness, while the train
whistled and whistled and finally
gathered up enough courage
to meet me.

Early Snow

He remembers this:
a teacher holding up
to the class
a piece of paper
on which he'd written
an answer so far
away from the truth
that the teacher's hand
could barely connect
with the sheet. And
the paper drifted
to the floor.
Outside it was snowing.

He remembers the snow
because he looked out
the schoolroom windows
as though that answer
had nothing to do with him,
and he remembers precisely
how that snow fell:
too white and thin
to take hold
of the red leaves
on the ground, or to
cover them.

The Supervisor

Hungover, at seven
in the morning, I fool
around at the machine
Joe is fixing, fumble
here and there with
the metal buttons, tease
the lever arm. My supervisor
comes over, yells at me,
says do you want to
start that big die plate
crashing down, do you want
to kill Joe? I am just
a dumb girl, eighteen,
and the supervisor is a man
I was out with last night,
drinking beer at a table
while his right hand
with the two missing
fingers found my knee
and traced a design
on the tight denim.
The supervisor bends
his head to the work,
his hair has streaks in it
like an old lady's fingers
running through it, his skin
under the blush of anger
is gray as lead, as gray
as his hair. I think,
I am eighteen, and can
still get out of here.

The Act of Eating a Whole Black Radish

cracked glove
on a cocked fist

Harley bars
let out all their leather
in one wet breath

exhaust
night, and then neon
you can taste:

the hot
white light is cruising
through your teeth

Two

Stewardess

Breakfasting on the best
cheesecake in the world
at Bernie's deli,
I was my daddy's sweetheart,
sweet as the green grass.
Now I carry

my trays down the aisles like any
waitress, and sometimes in May
when I fly over Wisconsin,
the green down there is tight
as the uniform

my taste for sweets
is making impossible,
tight as the ribbon
I used to wear
every Sunday for my daddy
in my fine waving hair.

Grandma

Grandma used to sit
and smoke
bring clouds onto the porch
talk and talk.
I searched through
Sears Catalogs cutting out
boys in their best suits
to be my sons
while I listened
listened until the dark came
and I put my children
to bed in a cigarette carton
then followed the lit end
of her Lucky up the stairs like
a doll-size moon
she had pulled down for me.

Her stories
were good clothes handed down
that I grew out of fast
into cars, older boys
and roads like rollercoasters
with the moon
big and ragged in the windshield
and she
slowed down so
that the stairs were whole days
with only the boring
tick, tick, tick of her feet
climbing in the quiet.

For years now I have been dreaming
of her sitting
in a room far away
where the shades

are stained with smoke and drawn out
like grieving
while she waits for just one more round
of gossip by the small light
of her imperfect granddaughter's
love
bright and brief as an adolescent's dress
on a dark porch.

Sideshow

Once I saw a woman as big as the world.
The chair couldn't contain her, the circus strained
to hold her. I was sure her ears were too
fat to hear, her eyes too fat to see.
I stared. And I whispered. Now I imagine
the baby like some monstrous bud expanding
in my belly, or an eager spectator elbowing me
out of his way in a stifling tent, and I remember
how, when the fat woman's tears fell,
they looked as heavy as pears, and as succulent.

Moon Money

One huge arc.
A child howls at
the gaping air
and a father keeps
to his own terrible orbit
of the swing set
shouting shut up, stay up
there be brave: what

a weird cosmology
that makes the sun
a man and the moon
female. Not on this playground.
Not on the psychiatrist's
couch where sagas
of cold distant fathers
unfold as night
follows day. And according
to Freud, this is almost
necessary–a boy has to
identify with his father
become a link in the long
metal chain and pull
away from his mother
or be drawn down
into confusion, collide
with love like a burning
consuming surface,
melt: so the man

in the park bribes his son
into not falling, into not
feeling how it felt,
falling, with a hard

shiny coin of candy
called Moon Money
and the boy peels back
the silver wrapper
and pays cash
this morning to shadows
circling, circling his
hushed tongue.

Cave Painting

My week-old daughter's
furious mouth

draws me inside
the cramped, dim walls

like a worshipped animal
who must be hunted down

her heartbeat a chant
her hand finding

emptiness
and then my outline.

Mother in the Park

Her children could drown
when the summer sky
flashes through the branches
as it does now, like a buffed
fin of the car
owned by her husband
as a teenage beau,
all those no's
cast into the dark
back seat as useless
as the little silver hooks
the children beg
to throw again and again
into the stream through
this same park where they catch
another sunset while she lugs
them and the equipment
home, the swing of
a bait pail filled with pretend
dinners and tiny deaths
at her hips,
words of love tugging
at the corner of her badly
lipsticked mouth.

Bride

He asks to use your phone
his car broke down
you are kneeling
on your soft green lawn
weeding the flowerbed
your little bit of pride
and you look up. The sun
is behind his head
blinding you, but you're sure
his face is unscarred
his height medium, his build
medium. You have been
groomed all your life for
this day, more important
than your wedding, whiter
than that, glaring
the hot bulb of the huge
camera going off,
illuminating your kitchen
which contains no trace
of dust. You peel off
the canvas gloves, pat
your hair in place, sigh,
notice how the hedges
will silence any witnesses
and lead him through
the already open door.

Make Wine

Let the grapes grow in the backyard
of your house untended. Then notice
them on a day when divorce
is mentioned. Enlist your husband,
dress your daughter in his old shirt
so she can pluck his heart.
Pick and pick and then press
against everyone in the kitchen,
appear reckless and happy, smash
grapes, make the pure porcelain sink blush
with joy, permanently. Add yeast, sugar
and raisins, but have too little
of everything so you can steal
from your daughter and wink
sinfully over her head at your husband.
Fill a laundry pail with purple,
let it sit in the front hall until
the sour smell sinks
into every thread of your one
good coat. Drag the bucket
into the basement. For three weeks
argue, slam doors, neglect
your daughter and then clasp
her to you at odd hours
with tears in your eyes. Remember
the wine. Find an angry froth
of dead flies and sloughed fruit
adrift in the liquid, skim it off,
funnel what's left into the cool embrace
of glass. Instantly desire
more breakage, but envision
a future filled with more waste,
more woe. Stand the upright
beautiful bottles in blood red rows.

Sharks

Once, out back, where
we always ran, we found
and surrounded a small boy,

an outsider. We taunted
him into climbing
an electric pole. When he hit

the wire, he jerked
like a swimmer pulled under,
then fell, scraping the lights

right out of the sky
for miles. Now I force
my four-year-old daughter

into the angry, shoving
crowd at Sea World
so that she will see and admire

those sharks, who are born
tireless, with a full set
of teeth and nothing to learn.

Wheat Field

Standing in a field of wheat,
I held my child's head to the hollow
of my throat. Light grew
from the ground, was brushing
our cheeks with bright strokes.
And in the whole scene, my daughter's
dark hair was the only dark thing.

Dead Ducks

My friend's husband weighs down
the couch at four o'clock
in the afternoon, drunk again.
My friend and I talk about pawning
wedding rings, then we take
the kids to the duck pond.
A new sign warns against
feeding the birds, so greedy
they eat until they die.
We toss bread into the water anyway.
What are a few dead ducks
compared to our children's joy?

From Shore

For a week, we live
in the sagging cabin
near the lake. They clear

no beaches here.
Still, the children
are attracted

on a hot day
to the rank, brown surface
of the water.

I sit on shore
while a boy and girl,
both ten, viciously

and surreptitiously splash
my daughter, who is
much too young to swim

on their terms. But she keeps on
paddling after them
like a small dog

hopeful, awkward,
faithful. The sun
beats down on my back

and tires me like the red
wine I drink with Rita
on the porch back home,

hearing her ruin
the life of a good neighbor
with her sweet, sharp tongue

while I say nothing,
and I shout out no warning
now, because I love

what is wicked
just enough to have
earned this scene.

Dr. Egg

1 Married to Bandages

In Dr. Egg's waiting room
I meet a woman married
to bandages.

She says she is a good cook.
And I can see her standing
by the sink,
paring her white wrists
into a dark soup.

I smile at her and her smile back
is a bright knife

as she fondly undoes
the wrappings around her arms,
shows me the scars
she's raised
like babies.

2 Crime Scene

It is like an old movie
in this room,
1940s grainy
with a detective
and one witness who is also
a suspect.

The two enter an old house,
the wreck
of some good family's hopes,
night like ragged
curtains
at the windows.

The crime scene
is lit by a single match
in the shaking hand
of the witness seeing
what lingers
under the dust sheets
in the rotten plush
of the air
while the detective
pushes on

on into the next reel
until the film breaks,
flaps,
and the white
flickering light
reveals
Dr. Egg on the edge of his seat

and me tapping
my cigarette hard
on the edge of his ashtray,
smoke
curling around my wrist
like a handcuff.

3 Session 25: Chicken Killing

I follow my father
out to the chopping block.
He chases a chicken
in an unfair race
and forces
its head down to the wood.

Then blood is raining
into his pockets
shiny as candy or money
and he hoists
the skinny body up the trunk
of his arm
until it touches the sky.

At night I peep
out of my blanket
and all the stars in my window
are twitching
like small, involuntary muscles.

4 Dr. Egg's Wife

I send Dr. Egg
47 poems in a loose-leaf notebook.

At the next session
he says he likes them.
The room fills up
with all the details
he doesn't add.

One day I see a woman
walking out of his office.
The hard heels of her boots prick
at the linoleum
like an argument.

I go in and Dr. Egg
is shuffling the pages of my notebook.
Is that your wife? I ask.
He acts
as though I've seen a mirage.

5 Security

In the waiting room
I snag bits
of the big news,
how they found a doctor lying
in a pool of white paper,
and the patient just
aimlessly
swinging an emptied gun.

When I walk in on Dr. Egg,
he is fumbling
with some forms on his desk.
I reach for
my pocket.
His hand jumps
into his opened drawer

and for that split second
we are worse
than strangers:
I pull out my pen and offer it.
He pulls out
nothing.

6 I Imagine the Death of Dr. Egg's Daughter

Dr. Egg is walking her
down the path by the park,
the red leaves
making conversation
with her wheelchair.

He is listening
with his professional ears,
his father's heart,
and hears it coming
that minute
like a pack of dogs
bursting out of the trees.

He tries to outrun it,
pushes her
over rocks, the lumpy grass,
no sound from his daughter
during this hard ride.

Then the metal handles
are so light
they slip
right through his fingers.

7 Dr. Egg on Indefinite Leave

He takes off
like a married man
who goes down to the drugstore
for a pack of cigarettes,

suddenly sheds his life
in the street
like a coat,
disappears into the hot night,

leaves behind
all my unasked questions,
his young children
marooned in their sleep.

8 The Poem

I stand by the magazine rack.
The clerk is selling toothpaste.
Outside the plate glass, the day
is unraveling in snow.

There is snow on the page
of the magazine and tracks
that lead to a poem.
The light in the drugstore

is the same light
they have in the hospital.
I pull gently on the poem
and it follows my hands.

I press it under my shirt
like a bandage.

Happy

The house was perfectly silent,
the silence broken only
by the breathing of my sleeping
daughter, and the wind,
the cool wind of evening which rushed
in through the open window and over
me until I trembled like a dry
leaf after an outburst of rain.
I was happy then, perfectly happy,
so happy I couldn't concede it was
happiness, and called it anything else:
daughter, cool wind, open window, silence.

Back to Make the Bears Sick

I saw a big trashy
tangled blonde family
feed marshmallows
to the bears. The daddy
stood right by the sign
saying no to it
and nudged the wife
below the halter top,
in the tender part
that overflowed her jeans
when the bears sat up,
clapped, looked fat
and begged for more.
One kid tried to climb
over the railings
and got whapped up
the side of his head
and the other ones began
to wail and their noses
ran green and I could tell
their grievances
would be perpetual
and that they'd cling
like wet sugar
to this one afternoon
and bring their own
bony children back
to make the bears sick.

Three

Evelyn Nesbit in Minnesota

The cornstalks
weave in and out of the broken wheels.
The rust of the wheels turns blue and gold
under the twisted flowers.

The famous beauty
rides past fields and junkyards
into the narrow
main streets of the small northern towns:

the men she passes
suddenly do not recognize their wives
in the women beside them

and the women mistake their husbands,
who, looking,
have become so handsome.

Spring

Rain swells
the houses into soft, voluptuous postures.
The ground springs back to our touch
like cake, we smell spring
in the damp sheets. We trim
our clothes back like hair,
walk out with our shirts open. The throats
of birds singing are black
peepholes pricked in the gray air.
We want to abandon
our marriages and sin sweetly
in the treetops. Nature knows what
we think, goes on weaving
love like a blanket, the sun
a white spider in the morning sky.

Matchstick Romance

a husband beats
his wife methodically
like it's a job
he doesn't even pull the shades down

every so often
her red hair flares in the window
like a matchhead
popped up out of the book

it's been three years
since he showed her that trick
tucking down the cover
so that one stick stood up

in a certain way
a dirty joke
and she laughed
throwing back her head

so that the whole neighborhood saw
the natural roots of her hair
blazing, setting off
an alarm they couldn't hear

Arlette

Arlette believes
that Elvis lives on.

Her big house is a shrine to him
and it takes one beer
per room to clean
all the memorabilia,
including the frame
which holds a handkerchief
his sweat once stained.

She swears that, on an evening
when her husband was being insulting,
Elvis appeared
as a giant fireball
which crossed her living room carpet
but did not singe it.

Her husband sits one bar stool
away from her now
for fear that in a hot
ecstasy of memory
she will reach out
with her powerful polishing arm,
and with a single swat,
send him flying.

The Physical Therapist

In one room, the physical therapist
manipulates the child's legs.
In another, the child's mother

plays Christmas carols on the piano
and thinks that this apartment
is decorated in good taste.

The physical therapist's lover
who has picked out the furniture,
walks on the beach with a different

lover who is more to his taste,
weaker. Moving the bones
of another takes a strong back

and hands. The mother's hands span
the keys, and she is no judge,
but the piano might be out of tune,

and it is July and the music
jingles like a sleigh
over disappearing snow. The child

is patient, believing in
the sound of his mother
playing in the next room, harsh

but sweet as a bit of voluntary
movement. If the physical therapist
looked out the window, he would see two lovers

kissing by the lake. But the view costs
so much per month, so he concentrates
on each small muscle, how it moves and connects

with others
under the skin
under his fingers.

Blood

She comes to the door
in her red kimono.
Says wrong
time of the month, Jack.
Shuts the door in your face.

Silk threads
of rage begin to weave
through the whites of your eyes.
Red threads.
The same red.

Foreign Woman Boarding a Train

A woman lifts her child
in one arm. Her slim
departure is like a stem
pushing through the black earth. Suns
are simply rising and falling
halfway around the world again
with small, fierce gestures.
The perfume of decampment breaks
from her silk dress and she folds
the night at the end of the station
into her yellow pleats,
leaf after dark leaf.

J. Paul Getty III: Two Sonnets

Italian flair of one dark moment:
the sharp knife in a kidnapper's hands
parts the air then the hair on the bent
head, a light crust of blood settles on strands
of yellow, fine as petals, his cruel
grandpapa finds the ear like a sea
shell in a gift box with the life tooled
out of it. The power of money
to hack at the body bears some
resemblance to love and you wear
young Getty's trembling on your handsome
body like a rich man's suit with a tear
in the pocket, the hard coin of bliss
beats at your skin whenever we kiss.

Ten years more. J. Paul Getty III, ransomed
for a long time, and long time abuser
of severe substances, is now blind,
speechless, confined to a wheelchair,
confined to a paragraph in another man's story,
borne on the shoulders of strong paid men
through an L.A. hot spot, his bare ruined body
barely news, ten lines in a magazine
slick as sweat on the skin after love.
We stick like pages of that glossy paper
inert as money, unable to move
apart, joined in a little whisper
the fading sightless heir might hear
underneath the music with his remaining ear.

Unnatural Appetites

When Van Gogh was painting his stars,
he took just a taste of paint. It burned.
His hot throat turned inside out
and took in the night, the tree, the dirt.
He spit back the landscape unnaturally
on the canvas, and went to a blue

café with his buddies. A blue
green glass of absinthe with stars
of toxins in its depths naturally
flowered inside his hand. It too burned
going down, reaching the roots, the dirt
heart of Van Gogh. Absinthe is made out

of wormwood from which terpene reaches out
to intoxicate. It's in turpentine too. Van Gogh, blue,
would try to drink turpentine, thinner of dirty
colors into something clearer, like stars.
What was this hunger which burned
Van Gogh's night away, gave him this unnatural

artist's appetite? Pica, a depraved craving for unnatural
food, is not so uncommon. It turns out
that many men eat real nails for breakfast. The burning
desire of pregnant women, big as the blue
sky in wrinkled maternity dresses is for stars
of laundry starch. And kids eat dirt

when, in their bare yards, there's only dirt
to graze on. Maybe Van Gogh's essential nature
was to eat paint thinner. And he became such a startling
painter because of his desire to dine out
on an artist's actual tools, the blues
and yellows and reds on his palette. And the burning

talent was only a strange hunger which burned
through to the next world too: in the dirt
of his grave, a thuja tree, true blue
source of the toxic element in absinthe, naturally
grew down and set its roots out
to twine around Van Gogh's coffin. You might start

early to deny the burning of whatever you desire unnaturally.
Still, you never get the dirt out of the starved kid.
And the blue sky arches forever, painfully pregnant with stars.

The Cloud Forests of Sumatra

"The fire, two towns away,
was suspicious. Two children
died in it." Not ours,

thank God. The black and white
type crosses the newspaper page
like a line of innocuous ants,

not "the fire ants that stung
a sixty-year-old man to death
in Texas." No relation,

one more inheritance
we don't have to worry about.
"The cloud forests of Sumatra

are disappearing due to
global warming" and a man
down the block, in a hot

rage, narrowly missed
his wife with a bullet.
We never met, but if he'd

held that gun to my head,
I still couldn't have told
him where Sumatra is.

Hexasyllabics on Ted Bundy

"Capital punishment is our society's recognition of the sanctity of human life."
–Orrin Hatch

He liked them with dark hair
parted in the middle.
He liked them young. He'd nose
his car up to some street
corner where a small town sweetheart
waited as if
there were other nights left
and then drive off with her

into the sunset. I
saw a Dirty Harry
movie once, the first one,
the best, where the villain
buried a young girl for
ransom. The police dug
the body up in front
of the most beautiful

California dawn, and
the red, technicolor
sky outlined the outrage
of her tiny, limp shape.
It was such a perfect
representation of
wanton murder that we
all cheered when Harry threw

his badge away and shot
the man. Evil should be
so simple all the time.
Ted Bundy is one more
good example. After
ten years on Death Row, he
confessed to so many
murders that the surface

of America turned
foreign, pocked like the moon
with shallow graves. Who can
forgive him for what he
did to this image of
our lives? Why even his
mom would have been able
to forget the shining

Buddha face her son wore
into the cradle, and,
with the others outside
the prison selling T-
shirts, whooping at the sweet
flick of the switch, might have
loved, in her empty heart
that day, to see him fry.

Vietnam

You become pen pals with a convict.
It's not polite to ask what he's
in for, so you write about the weather.
He writes back about his tattoos,
how many there are and where.
When he's released, you meet him
at the bus station. You recognize
those big blue arms, fall into them
the way a letter enters an envelope,
and take him home. The house is in your name,
a big house on a bluff. Your husband
is a small man, and he loves the view
and has enough room for the first
time in his life, so he says nothing.
The three of you live like this for a long time.
Then you have a son. In the cradle
he waves his arms like flags.
You give a birthday celebration but none
of the guests come, except for your mother.
She shakes her head slowly over the debris
of the party, and says I don't understand
your generation and its arrangements. You
should have fought World War II
and we should have gone to Vietnam.

Joan of Arc at the Shopping Mall

God, who is good
with the ladies,
opens his arms
and says buy anything
at all
and Joan smiles
the muscles in her cheek
exposed
to show how a smile works
how miraculous

and she fits right in
with her short chic
haircut, parts
of it singed crisp
and a beautiful woman
with a basket
full of samples sprays
perfume directly
into the third degree burns
and Joan lifts her wrist
to sniff the scent
and orders a hundred
bottles on God's account

and in the food garden
on the third floor
Joan eats nothing
she gets nourishment
from the lights, the slick
displays of merchandise
and just being out with God
like this, in public.

At 31 Flavors

I wait with two other women
who came in first.
They are slim, neat.
I wait for the boy to serve them,
but they hesitate.
They hesitate and a man comes in.
He gets served next.
Now the women are ready,
but it's too late,
the shop has filled up
and I won't be polite,
it's already cost me
my turn, people are starting
to get served at random,
all order is lost.
It's a good excuse.
A fat, dilapidated woman and her dark-skinned
daughter at the end of the counter
wait and are ignored.
I take my cone out and sit on the curb.
I'm half done when
the big woman pulls her daughter
roughly through the door
and shouts "I wouldn't spend
my last fucking dollar in there."
A car full of men is waiting for them.
They get in. It roars away.
My ice cream tastes
like exhaust. I watch
the first two women
leave, looking innocent.

That's how all these things start.

Nothing to Eat

There is nothing to eat.

Just this apple.
Otherwise there is nothing to eat.

And some cake.
A little meat. Otherwise,
there is nothing to eat.

I forgot these tomatoes
but they aren't very red.
And the bread. But there is
nothing to eat.

Oh, and the fields of wheat laid out
state to state,
silos stuffed with grain
like turkey throats
and dairies and slaughterhouses,
milk and enough blood
for every sunset,

and the restaurants
with their bloated portions,
and the plates stacked
for washing with scraps
still clinging, and the garbage scows
towing the waste out to meet
the sea's unmoving depth.

Otherwise, there is nothing to eat.

Love

Let's say a space alien
comes down to herd
humans for food.

Let's say it is like
a young girl from the city,
moved to a farm

at her father's whim,
who feeding up, caring for a particular
representative of beef,

becomes fond of it.
Let's say, one night
before the slaughter,

the alien is stroking
the soft hair on a human's head,
let's say that its voice

sounds like the plane
approaching Hiroshima,
engines turning over as fast as possible,

let's say that it knows
what regret is,
that it is crooning:

I am something you have never
heard of, I am something
you don't want to know about.

Significant Other

In 1811, in Siam,
the birth
was smooth:
the head of one
fit exactly between
the legs of another
so that their course
into the world
was no worse
than a single child's.
It was not until
the midwife
took them to bathe
that the band
of flesh, thick
as a third arm
was found, binding
them together
at the chest,
and joy twisted
into horror.

They grew up, however,
as happy as children
usually were.
One slept
when his brother slept.
Neither would eat
what disagreed
with the other.
Once, running
on the ship
that was taking
them to America
to be displayed,

a hatchway opened
up at their feet,
and they safely leapt
over in perfect unison
when the least slip
of sympathy
would have meant death.

It is true
that as they grew older,
their differences
grew deeper.
Chang, the irascible
twin, drank more
and more, and Eng,
the quiet one, dreamed
of separation
so often that rejoining
the waking caused him
pain which Chang
drank more heavily day
after day to deny,
but don't we,

even though we are
repelled by all
the details
of their sex lives
and toilet habits,
the sheer difficulty
of beds and chairs
and stairways,
envy them
more than a little?
After all, to have

someone who must
move through the world
in the same awkward
way we do, bleed
when we bleed,
hover helpless
beside us in our fevers
and never leave or
divorce us, isn't this
what we wish
when we wish
people well in love?

Chang, the weaker
twin, died of a stroke
one night. Eng,
waking to find
his brother dead
in the bed beside him,
died of fright.

B. J. Buhrow lives in Milwaukee, Wisconsin, with her eight-year-old daughter Roxanne. Buhrow is a graduate of the University of Wisconsin-Milwaukee and the University of Wisconsin-Madison. She has worked at and relinquished many jobs over the last fifteen years—press operator, typist, industrial engineer, doctor's wife, newspaper reporter, and waitress in a restaurant that sold horsemeat sandwiches. Buhrow currently is a first-year law student and is working on a second book of poetry, *Great Sex Crimes of the Twentieth Century*.

About her writing, Buhrow says: "I write poems for the same reason (except money) that Judy Tenuta does stand-up comedy. I can't imagine my life otherwise."